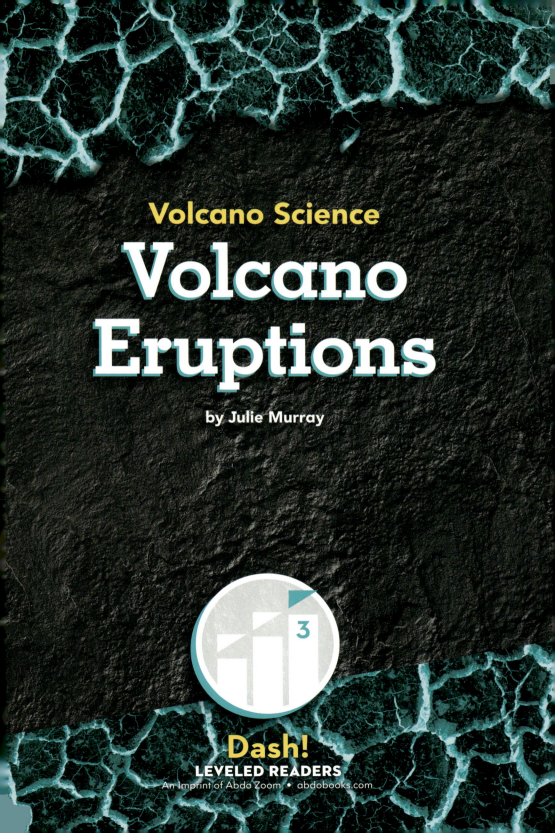

Volcano Science

Volcano Eruptions

by Julie Murray

Dash!
LEVELED READERS
An Imprint of Abdo Zoom • abdobooks.com

Level 1 – Beginning
Short and simple sentences with familiar words or patterns for children who are beginning to understand how letters and sounds go together.

Level 2 – Emerging
Longer words and sentences with more complex language patterns for readers who are practicing common words and letter sounds.

Level 3 – Transitional
More developed language and vocabulary for readers who are becoming more independent.

abdobooks.com

Published by Abdo Zoom, a division of ABDO, PO Box 398166, Minneapolis, Minnesota 55439. Copyright © 2023 by Abdo Consulting Group, Inc. International copyrights reserved in all countries. No part of this book may be reproduced in any form without written permission from the publisher. Dash!™ is a trademark and logo of Abdo Zoom.

Printed in the United States of America, North Mankato, Minnesota.
052022
092022

Photo Credits: Alamy, Getty Images, Science Source, Shutterstock
Production Contributors: Kenny Abdo, Jennie Forsberg, Grace Hansen, John Hansen
Design Contributors: Candice Keimig, Neil Klinepier

Library of Congress Control Number: 2021950303

Publisher's Cataloging in Publication Data

Names: Murray, Julie, author.
Title: Volcano eruptions / by Julie Murray.
Description: Minneapolis, Minnesota : Abdo Zoom, 2023 | Series: Volcano science | Includes online resources and index.
Identifiers: ISBN 9781098228415 (lib. bdg.) | ISBN 9781098229252 (ebook) | ISBN 9781098229672 (Read-to-Me ebook)
Subjects: LCSH: Volcanoes--Juvenile literature. | Volcanic eruptions--Juvenile literature. | Volcanism--Juvenile literature. | Physical geography--Juvenile literature.
Classification: DDC 551.21--dc23

Table of Contents

Volcano Eruptions 4

How Volcanoes Erupt 8

Volcano Dangers 16

More Volcano Facts 22

Glossary 23

Index 24

Online Resources 24

Volcano Eruptions

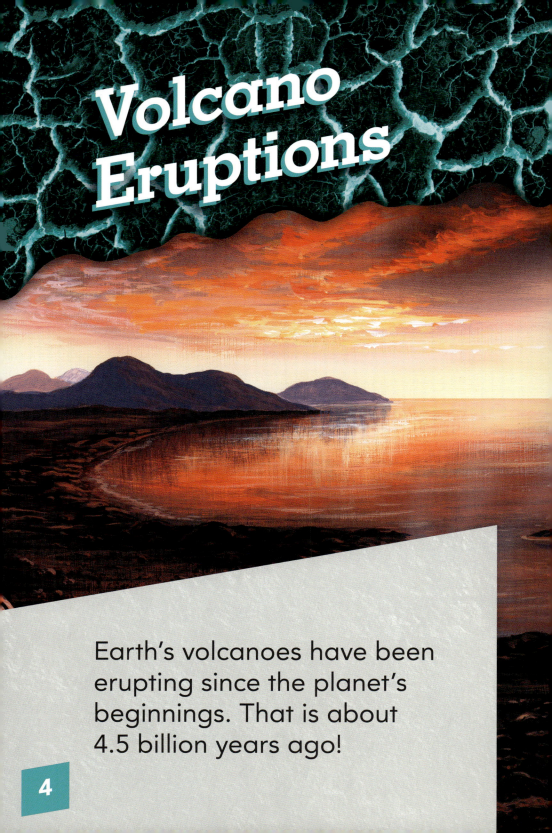

Earth's volcanoes have been erupting since the planet's beginnings. That is about 4.5 billion years ago!

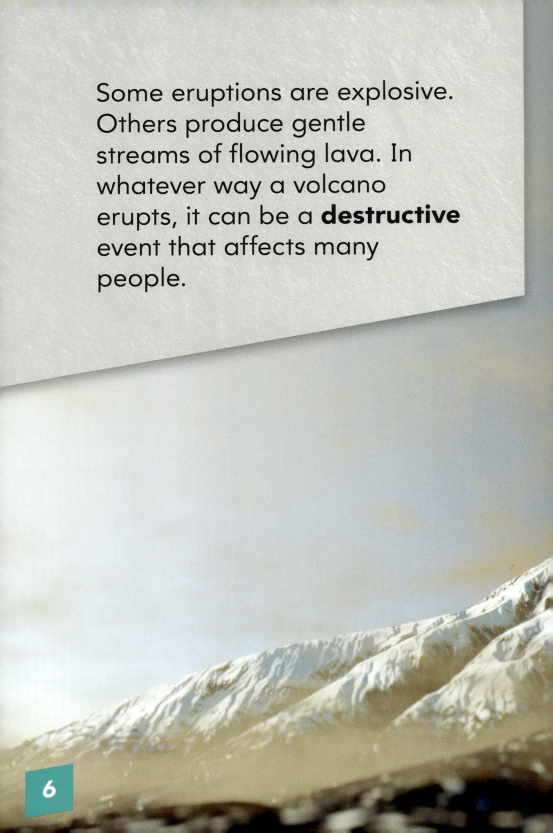

Some eruptions are explosive. Others produce gentle streams of flowing lava. In whatever way a volcano erupts, it can be a **destructive** event that affects many people.

How Volcanoes Erupt

Volcanoes erupt when magma rises to the surface. Magma is found deep inside the Earth. It is so hot there that rock melts into magma.

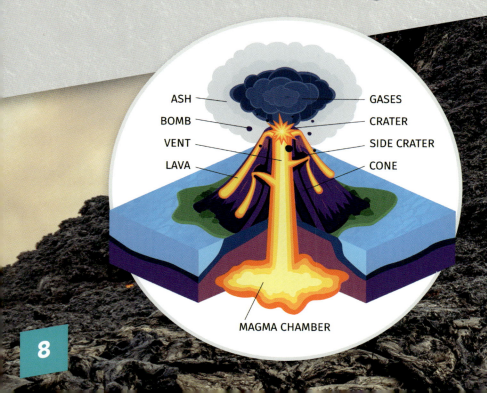

Magma rises because it is lighter than solid rock. It moves through cracks in Earth's **crust** and into a magma chamber. Over time, more and more magma enters the chamber.

The movement of magma builds up gases and creates enormous **pressure**.

Runny magma can escape more easily. Thick magma can get trapped, creating an explosive eruption.

Magma moves up the volcano's vent. It can escape through **fissures** and side craters, or through the main crater. Once at Earth's surface magma is called lava.

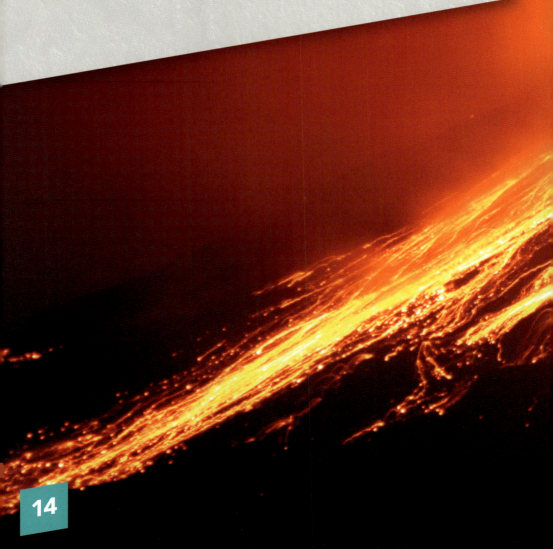

15

Volcano Dangers

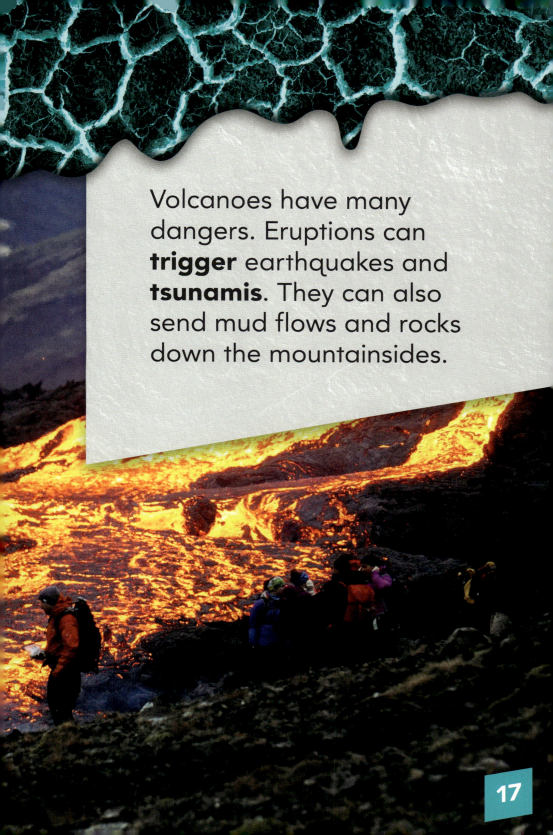

Volcanoes have many dangers. Eruptions can **trigger** earthquakes and **tsunamis**. They can also send mud flows and rocks down the mountainsides.

An entire town can be destroyed if it is near a volcano. People can also be injured or die from falling ash and gases in the air.

19

Around the world, about 570 people die from volcanoes each year. In the past 500 years, about 270,000 people have died from volcanic activity.

More Volcano Facts

- Volcanic eruptions can last for a few hours to thousands of years.

- Every day, 10 to 20 volcanoes erupt around the world.

- Large volcanic eruptions put lots of ash in the air, causing Earth's temperature to lower by several degrees.

- Lava temperatures can reach 2,000 degrees Fahrenheit (1,093°C)!

- Lava can flow up to 30 miles per hour (48 kph).

Glossary

crust – the outer layer of Earth.

destructive – causing complete ruin or destruction.

fissure – a crack in the Earth that sometimes leaks lava.

pressure – a steady force upon a surface.

trigger – to cause, begin, or set off.

tsunami – a very large, often destructive sea wave caused by an earthquake or volcanic explosion.

Index

ash 19

crater 14

dangers 17, 19, 20

Earth 4, 8, 11, 14

effects 6, 17, 19, 20

gases 12, 19

lava 6, 14

magma 8, 11, 12, 13, 14

magma chamber 11

vent 14

Online Resources

Booklinks NONFICTION NETWORK
FREE! ONLINE NONFICTION RESOURCES

To learn more about volcano eruptions, please visit **abdobooklinks.com** or scan this QR code. These links are routinely monitored and updated to provide the most current information available.